folk harp
Celtic Christmas

21 Carol Arrangements for Celtic Harp
by
Kim Robertson

CONTENTS

ISBN 978-0-634-01327-0

HAL•LEONARD®
CORPORATION
7777 W. BLUEMOUND RD. P.O. BOX 13819 MILWAUKEE, WI 53213

Visit Hal Leonard Online at
www.halleonard.com

A la Nanita Nana

Traditional Spanish Melody

♩ = 108

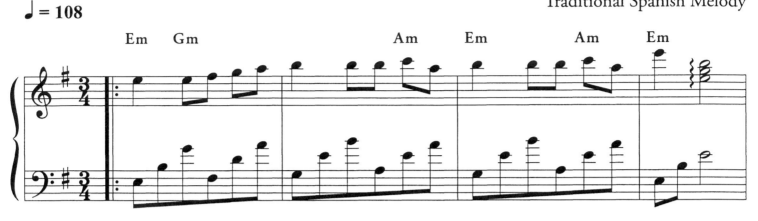

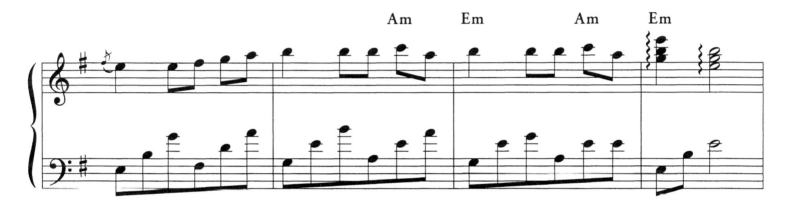

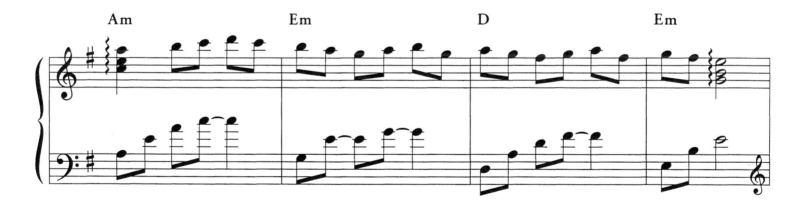

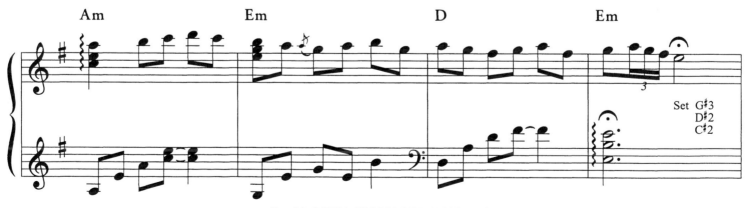

3

Away in a Manger

♩ = 76

William James Kirkpatrick

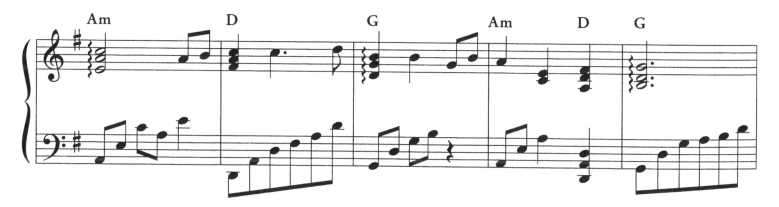

Christ Child's Lullaby

♩. = 40

North Hebrides

Intro.

Arpeggiate chords as needed throughout book.

(harmonics)

Interlude

Verse

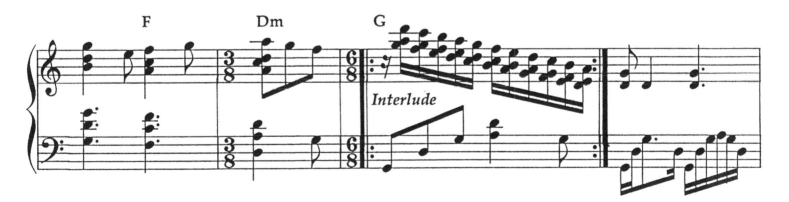

Verse (use fingernail)

Repeat and Fade

Come, All Ye Shepherds

Moravian Melody (1750)

♩ = 68

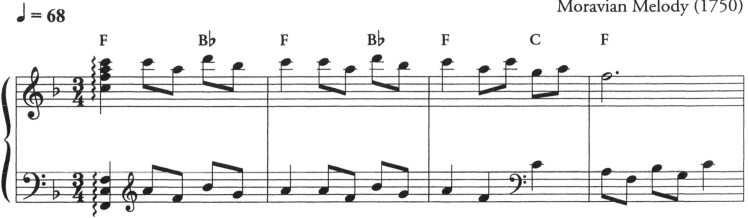

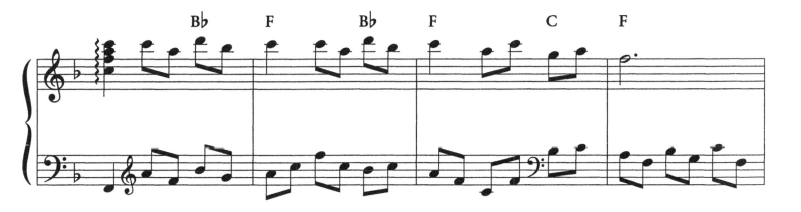

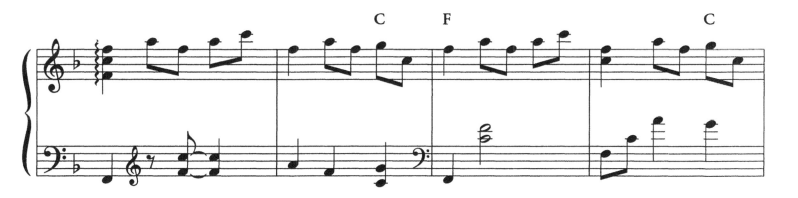

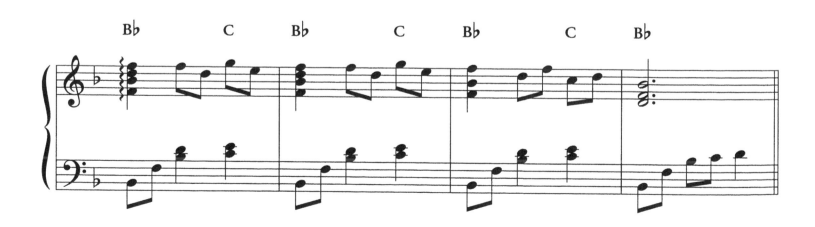

Coventry Carol

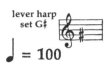 lever harp set G#

♩ = 100

England

Intro.

Verse

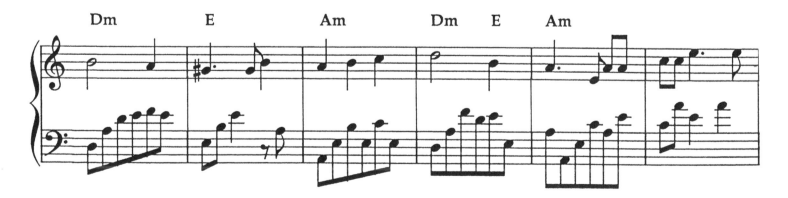

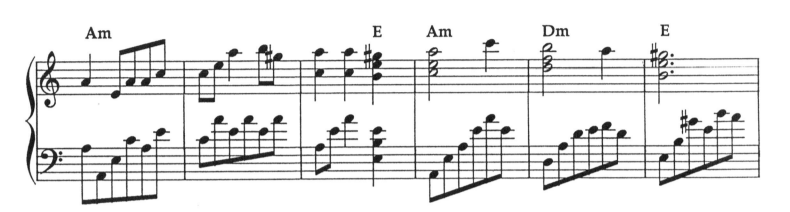

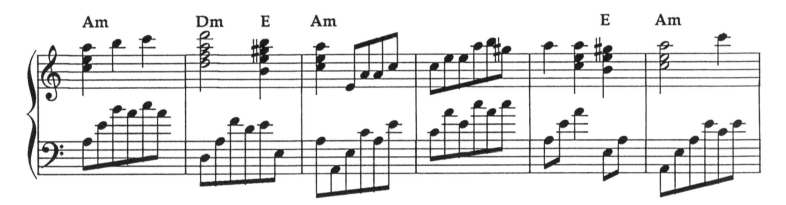

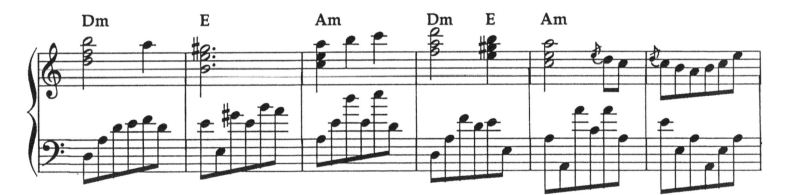

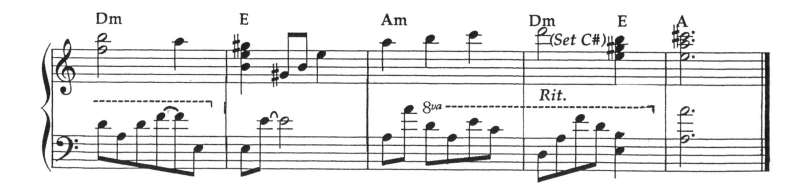

The First Nowell

♩ = 92

traditional

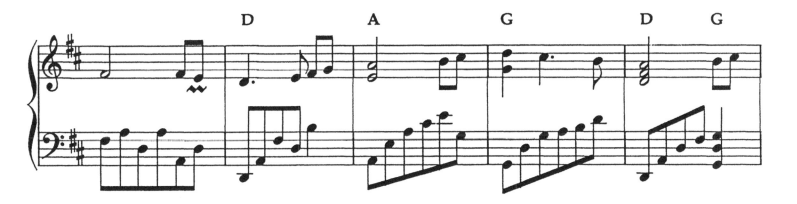

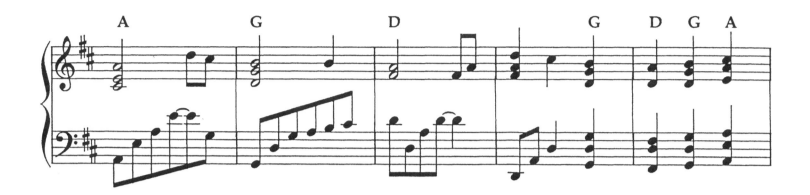

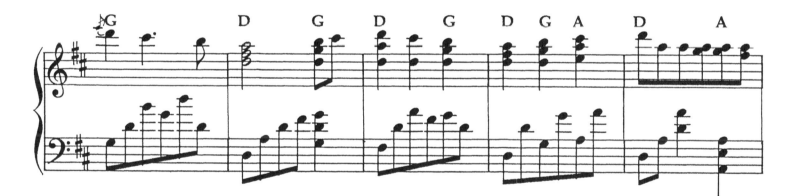

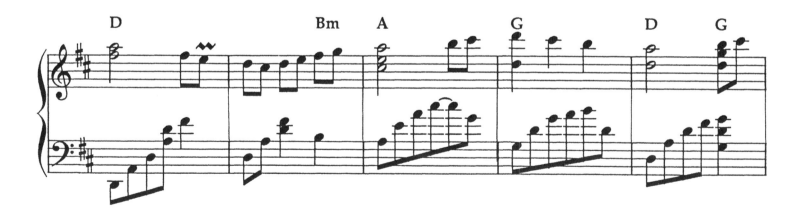

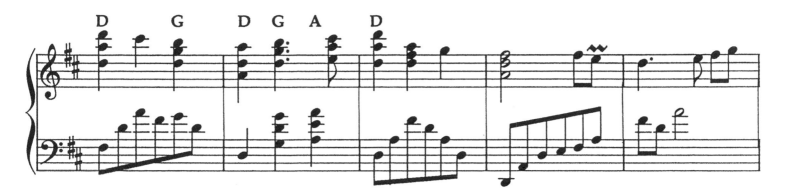

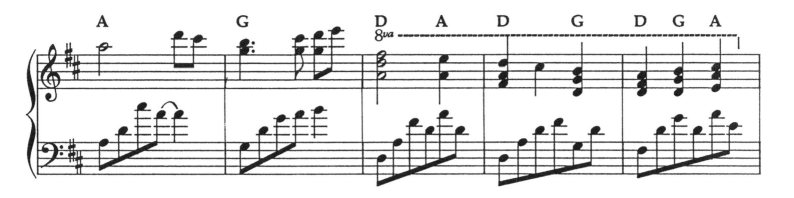

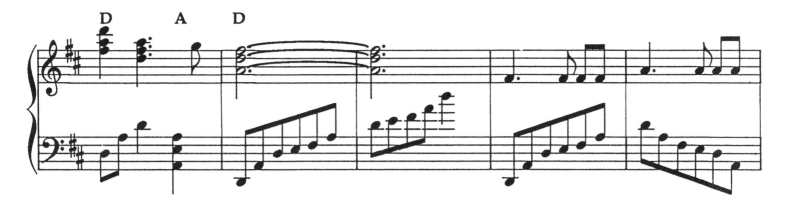

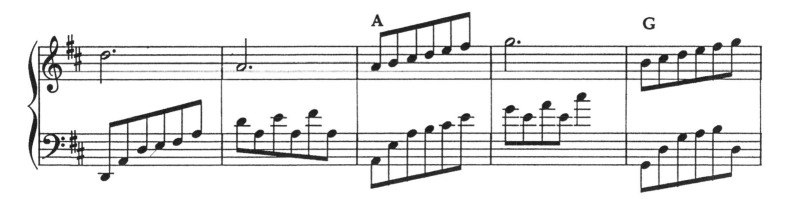

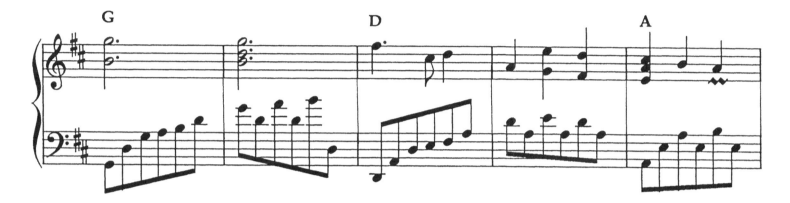

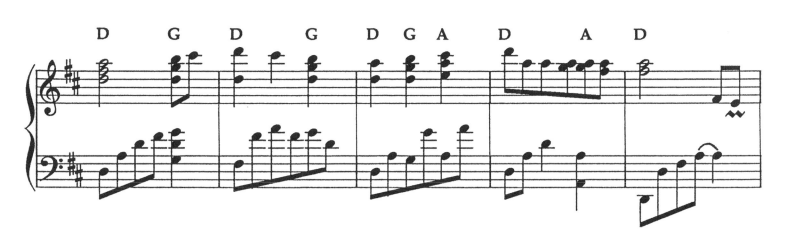

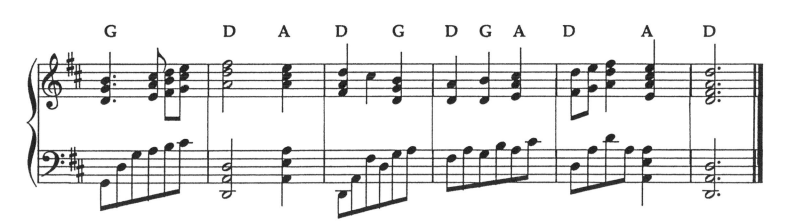

Ding Dong! Merrily on High!

♩ = 84

French Carol

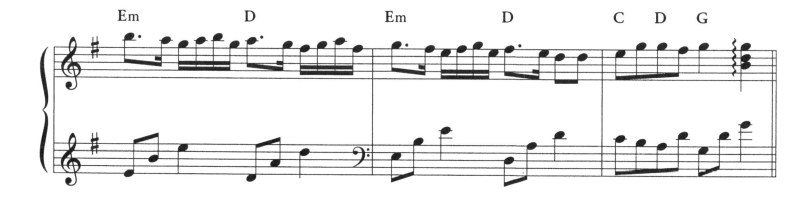

Divinum mysterium

♪ = 120

13th cent. plainsong

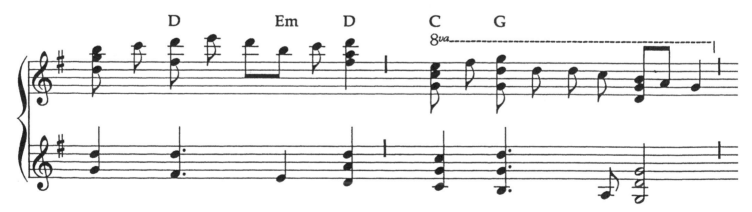

Entre le boeuf

♩ = 80

France

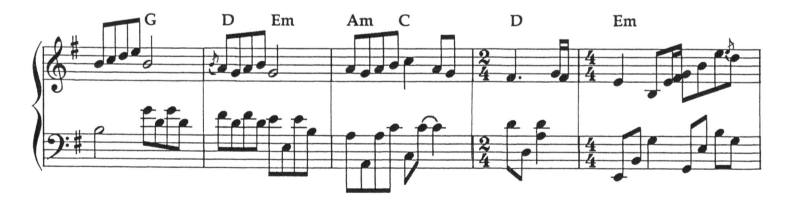

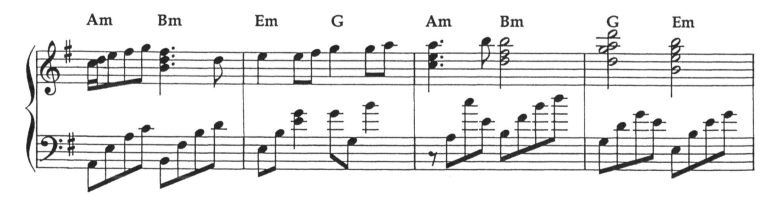

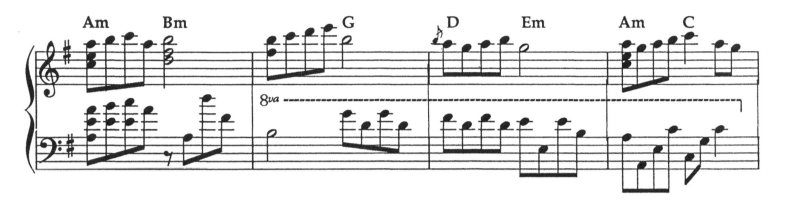

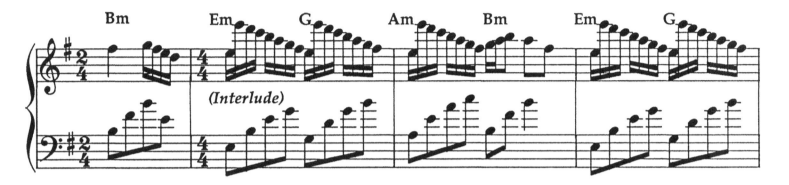

God Rest Ye Merry, Gentlemen

London melody
18th century

♩ = 256

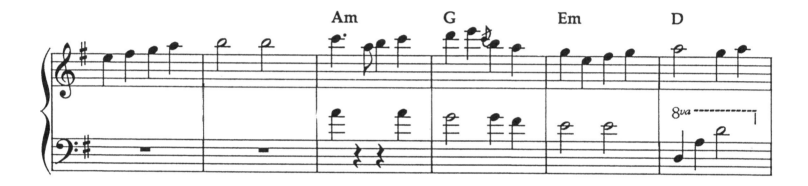

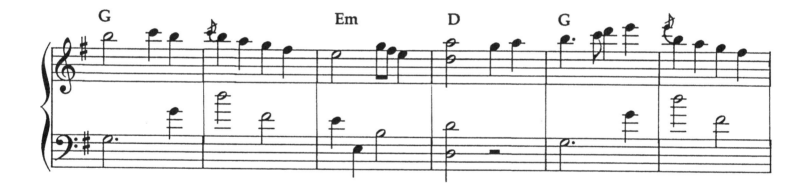

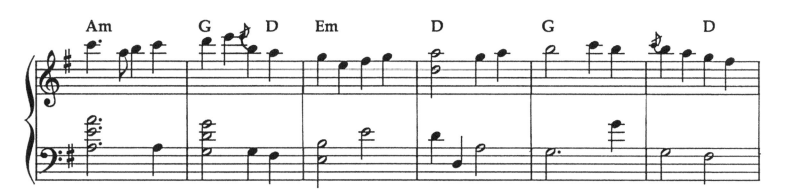

27

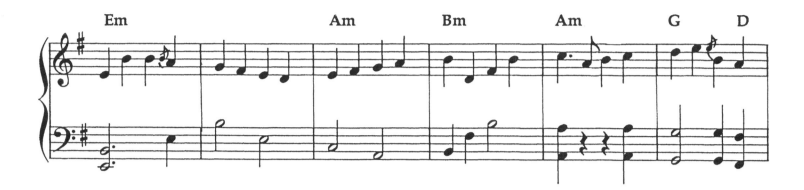

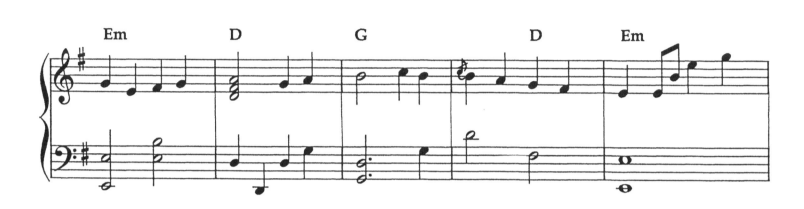

Good King Wenceslas

Andiam, mio tesoro medley

♩ = 168

Piae Cantiones 1582

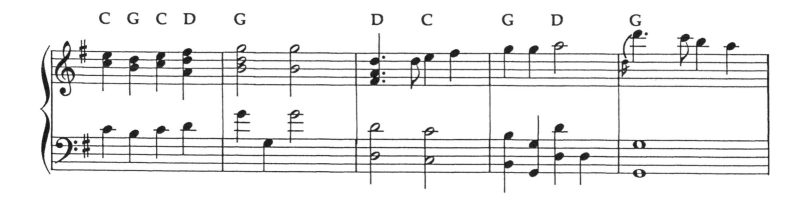

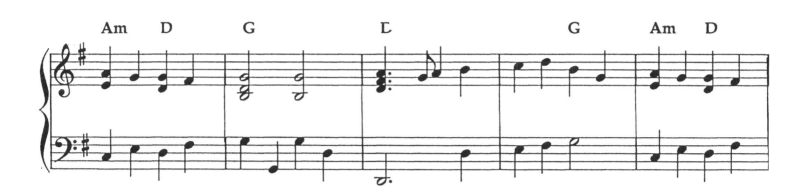

Rall. . . . .

Jesu, Joy of Man's Desiring

♩. = 80

J.S. Bach

Quand li bergié

♩ = 120

Avignon 16th cent. Bourrée

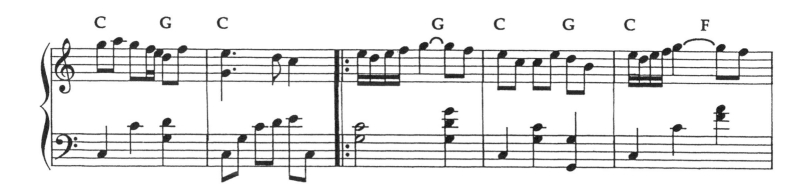

Rosa mystica
[Lo How a Rose]

♩ = 80

Germany

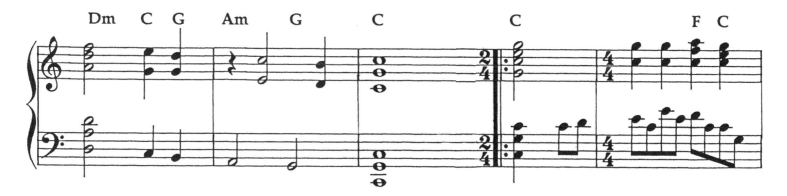

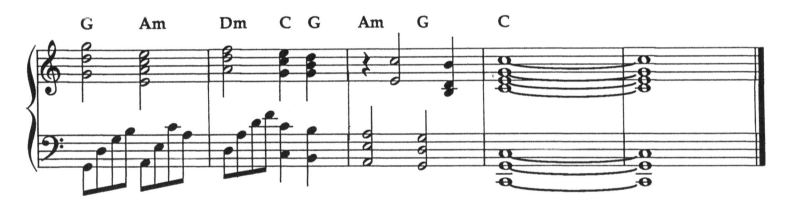

Saltarello

♩. = 72

Anon. Italy

G drone

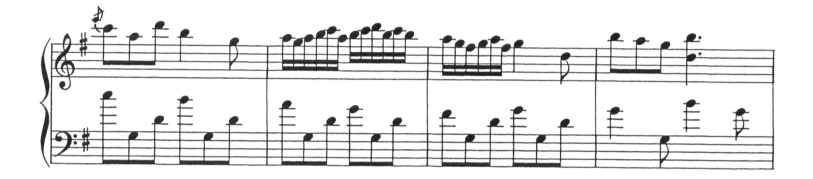

44

Sheep May Safely Graze

♩ = 76

J.S. Bach

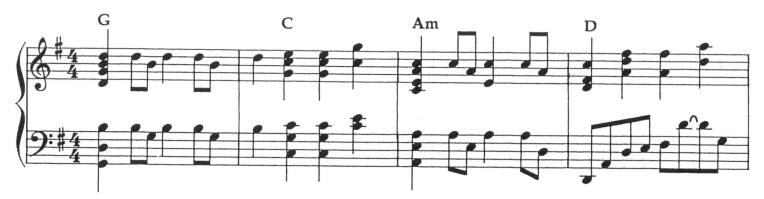

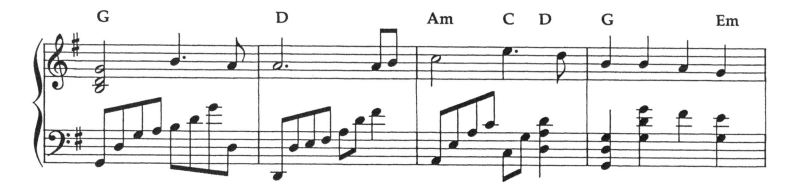

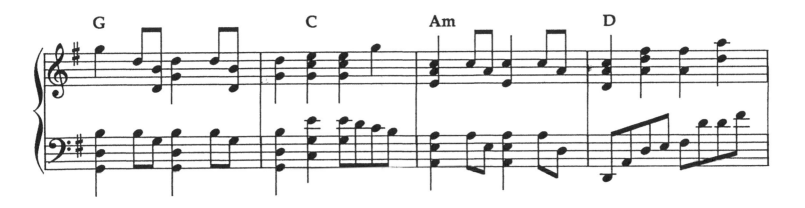

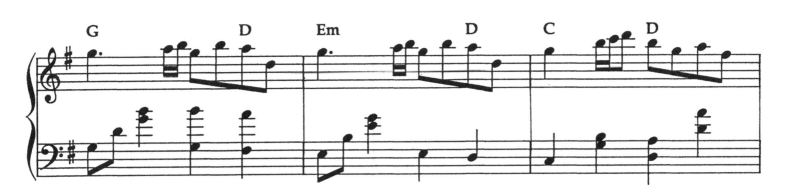

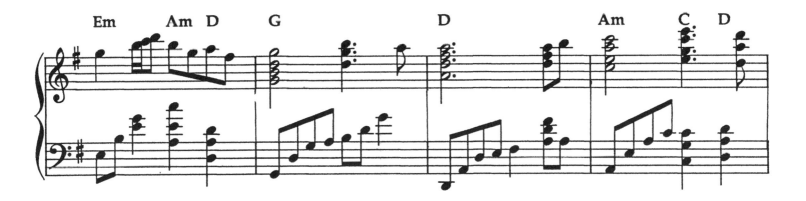

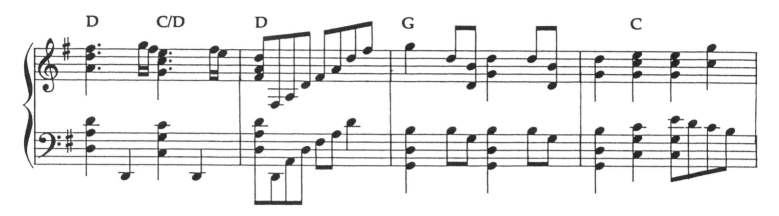

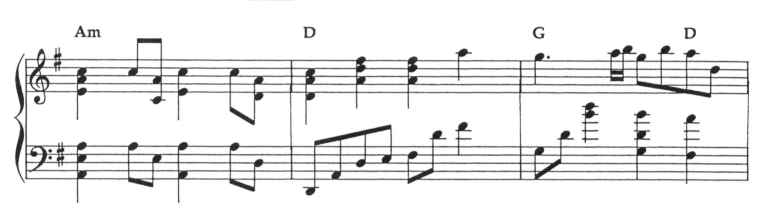

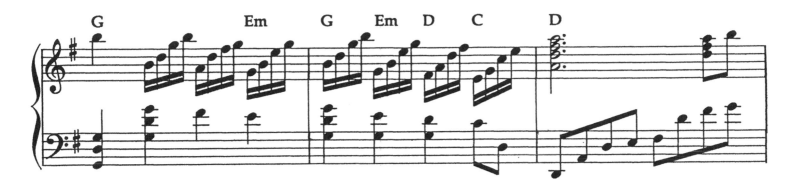

Silent Night

♪ = 84

Franz Gruber, 1818

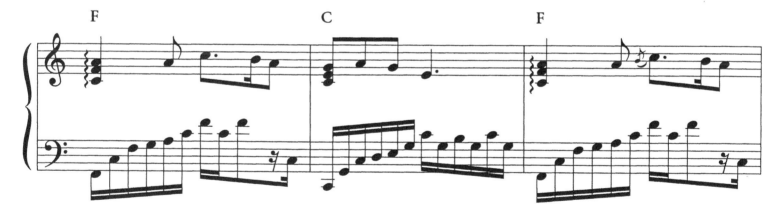

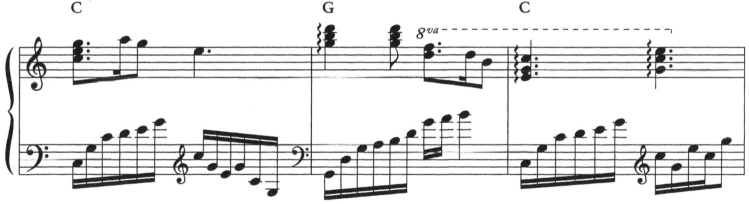

Veni Emmanuel

freely

plainsong

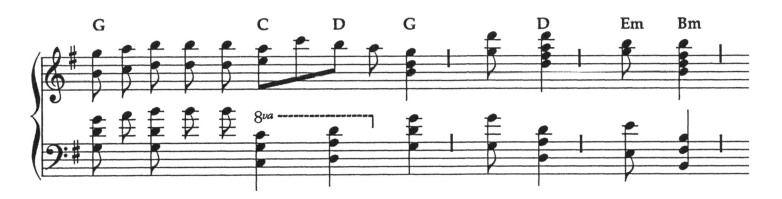

Venite adoremus

♩. = 120

traditional

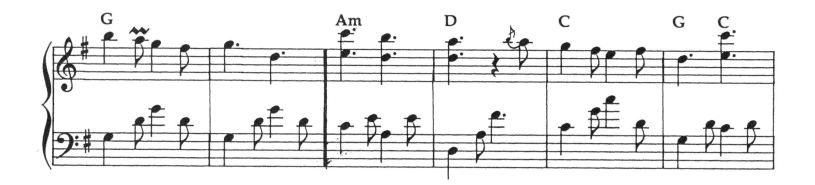

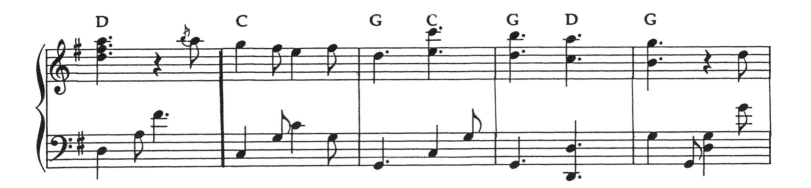

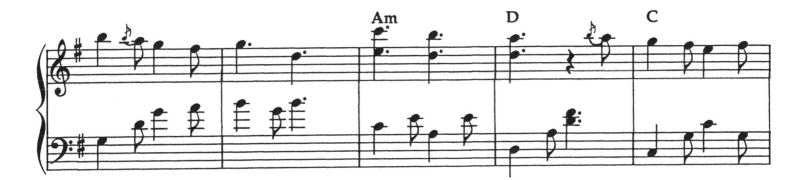

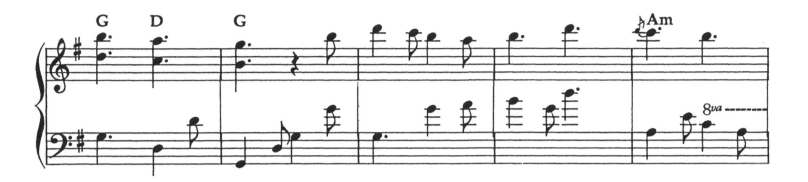

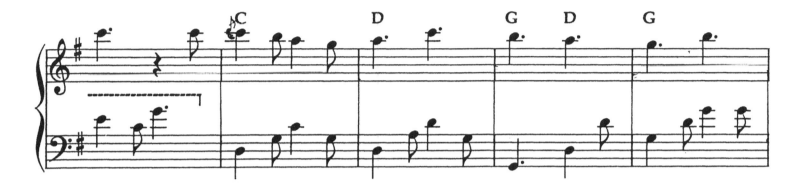

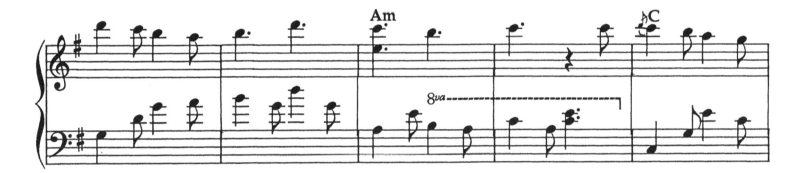

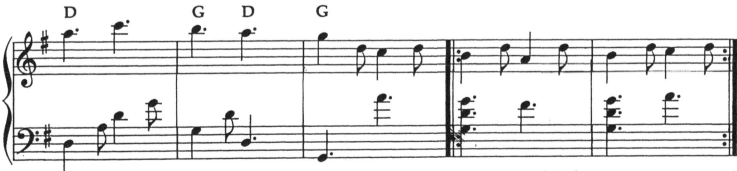

Repeat and Fade.

Verbum Supernum

Freely

Gregorian Chant

Greensleeves
[What Child is This?]

♩. = 40

traditional

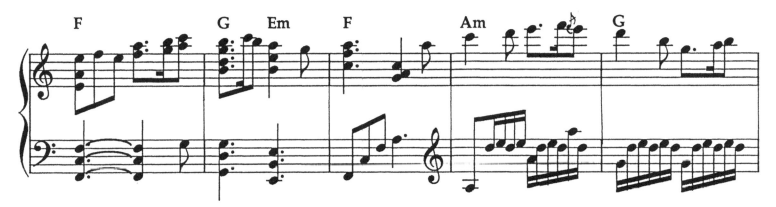

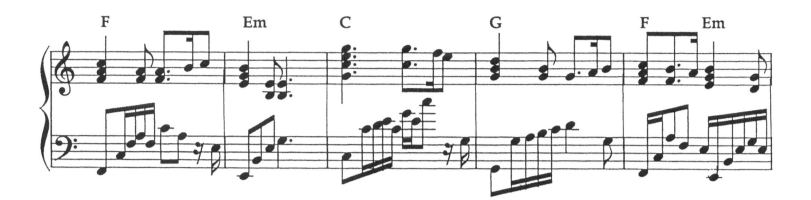

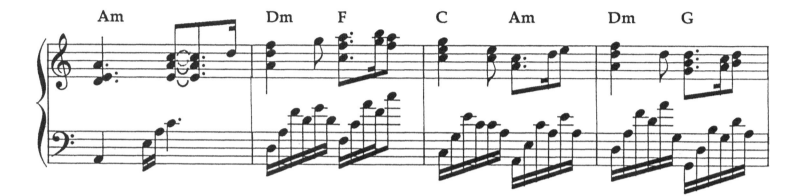

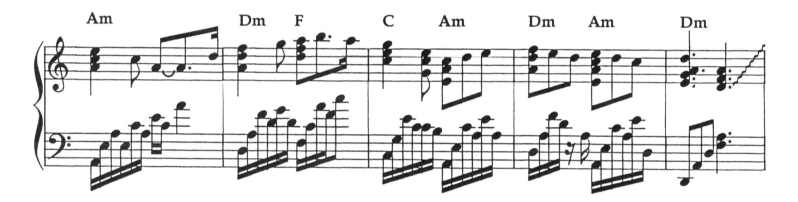

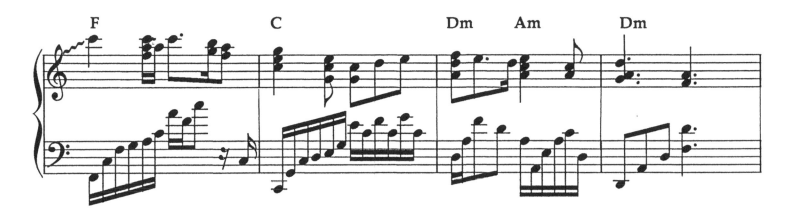

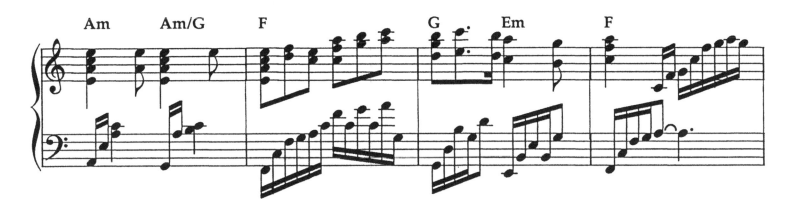

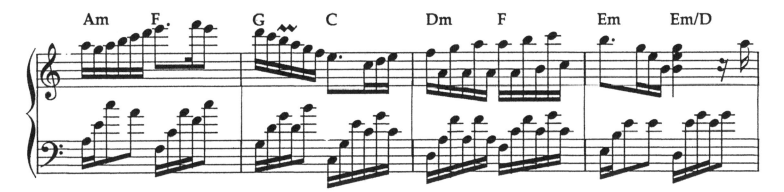

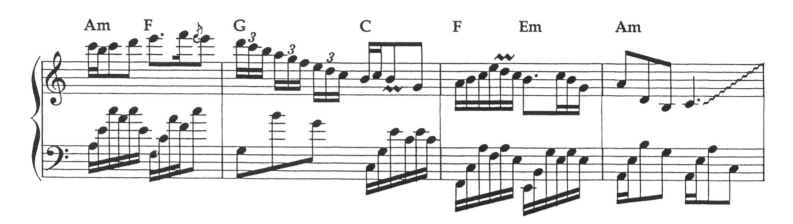

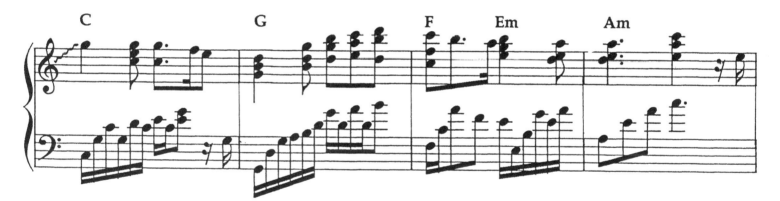

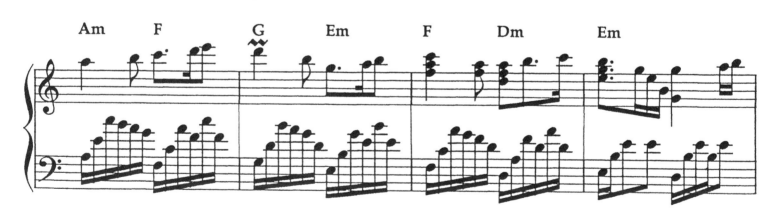

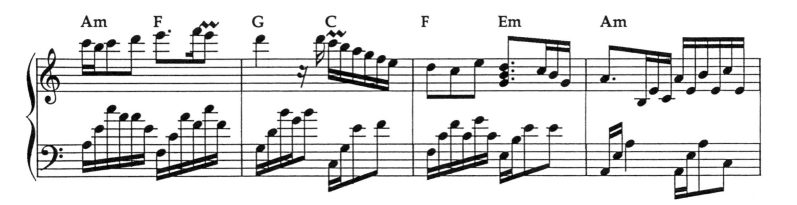

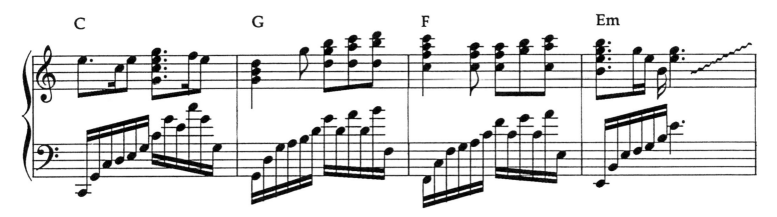

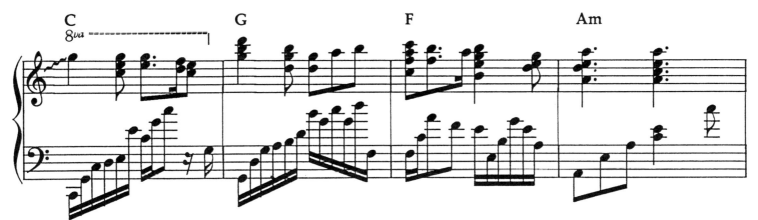

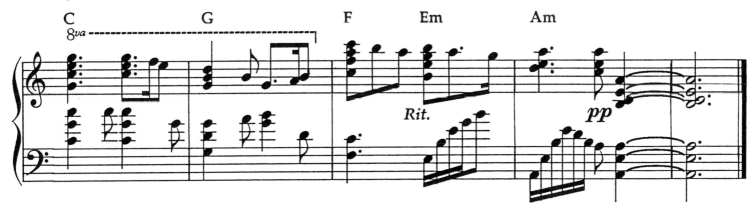

KIM ROBERTSON

Selected Discography

The Spiral Gate (Narada)
Treasures of the Celtic Harp (Dargason)
Wood, Fire & Gold (Dargason)
Tender Shepherd (Gourd Music)
Harvest Moon (Sugo)
Celtic Christmas (Invincible)
Celtic Christmas II (Invincible)
Windshadows II (Invincible)

Songbooks

Windshadows II (Hal Leonard)
Tender Shepherd (Mel Bay)
Celtic Harp Solos (Mel Bay)
Arranging for Harp (Mel Bay)
Treasures of the Celtic Harp (Mel Bay)

Videos

Treasures of the Celtic Harp (Mel Bay)
Beginning Folk Harp (Lark in the Morning)
Arranging for Folk Harp (Lark in the Morning)

For recent publications, contact:

Narada Productions
4650 North Port Washington Road
Milwaukee, WI 53212-1063